Children's Illustrators

Garth Williams

Jill C. Wheeler
ABDO Publishing Company

visit us at
www.abdopub.com

Published by ABDO Publishing Company, 4940 Viking Drive, Edina, Minnesota 55435.
Copyright © 2005 by Abdo Consulting Group, Inc. International copyrights reserved in all
countries. No part of this book may be reproduced in any form without written permission from
the publisher. The Checkerboard Library™ is a trademark and logo of ABDO Publishing
Company.

Printed in the United States.

Cover Photo: William Anderson
Interior Photos: Corbis pp. 7, 9, 11, 13; William Anderson pp. 5, 15, 16, 17, 18, 19, 21, 23

Series Coordinator: Jennifer R. Krueger
Editors: Kate A. Conley, Kristin Van Cleaf
Art Direction: Neil Klinepier

Special thanks to Mr. William Anderson for his help with this project.

Library of Congress Cataloging-in-Publication Data

Wheeler, Jill C., 1964-
    Garth Williams / Jill C. Wheeler.
        p. cm. -- (Children's illustrators)
    Includes bibliographical references and index.
    ISBN 1-59197-723-1
    1. Williams, Garth--Juvenile literature. 2. Illustrators--United States--Biography--Juvenile
literature. I. Title. II. Series.

NC975.5.W52W57 2004
741.6'42'092--dc22
[B]
                                                                          2004045088

Contents

The Eyes of the Author

Garth Williams is one of the most popular illustrators in children's literature. Many of the books he illustrated are now considered classics. Williams also wrote books of his own. However, he usually worked as the eyes of the author. His imagination made the words of others come to life.

Williams's real life was as vibrant as his illustrations. He was a world traveler. He studied art and **architecture** in several countries. He created lifelike portraits and elegant sculptures. He even dodged German bombs during **World War II**.

These experiences inspired Williams during his long career. He illustrated more than 100 children's books. They include favorites such as *Charlotte's Web* and *Bedtime for Frances*. He also illustrated the Little House series by Laura Ingalls Wilder.

Williams's success came from a combination of talent and curiosity. It seemed as if he could draw anything. This impressed author E.B. White when he and Williams worked on *Stuart Little*. White was delighted that Williams knew just what kind of shoes a mouse like Stuart would wear!

Garth Williams

An Early Artist

Garth Williams was born on April 16, 1912, in New York City. He spent his early childhood on a farm in New Jersey. He had one sister named Fiona. His father, Hamilton, was a cartoonist. His mother, Florence, worked as a **landscape** painter.

Having parents who were both artists deeply influenced Garth. He remembered that someone in his house was always drawing or painting. He grew up thinking that was the only job there was.

Garth's dad enjoyed telling the story of his son's first drawing. While sitting in a high chair, young Garth drew a pine tree on a steam-covered kitchen window with his finger. Hamilton then announced that his son was going to be an artist.

The young boy continued to show interest in drawing. One day, Garth sneaked into his father's studio. He found some cartoons his dad had been working on. Garth made his own additions to the cartoons. Hamilton declared once again that his son would be an artist.

As a child, Garth was also interested in music. He played guitar, piano, saxophone, and clarinet. Once he even learned a song just to impress a neighbor girl. His art, however, was more impressive than his music.

New York City in 1912 was crowded and busy. Garth was much happier on his family's New Jersey farm.

Art Student

Garth's family moved to England when he was ten years old. Garth wanted to become an **architect**. He thought it would be easier to get work as an architect than as an artist.

Garth found work as an architect's assistant in London. The job gave him the chance to explore some of the city's famous buildings. He also drew his own fantasy houses. They featured kitchens that automatically served food and washed the dishes.

But, the **Great Depression** put an end to Garth's plans. No one had the money to build expensive buildings anymore. The Williams family scraped together enough money to send Garth to art school for three months instead.

Garth attended Westminster Art School. Later, he earned a four-year scholarship to London's Royal College of Art. His specialty was creating portraits and sculptures.

Garth graduated from art school in 1934. He took a job as **headmaster** of the Luton Art School outside of London. However, he soon quit because the job did not leave him much time for his own art.

Garth needed money. So, his old sculpture instructor urged him to enter the 1936 British Prix de Rome sculpture competition. It was just six weeks away at the time. Amazingly, Garth won the contest. The award allowed him to live and study in Italy for free for two years.

Students paint at the Royal College of Art in 1931, the same year Garth attended.

Caught Up in the War

While in Europe, Williams met Gunda Davidson. The two married in 1939 and lived in London. Gunda found work as an interpreter for an American business. Williams took a job working on a new magazine for women. But **World War II** put an end to the magazine.

Williams had to find a new job. He began working with the British Red Cross on an ambulance crew. In 1940, German **dictator** Adolf Hitler ordered his bombers to attack London. Williams and other Red Cross workers collected the dead and injured from city streets.

This was a dangerous job. Williams saw one of his friends killed right at his side. Another time a bomb landed right beside Williams and injured his spine. The injury forced him to resign from the Red Cross.

Before becoming injured, Williams had made plans for his family. He had sent his wife and daughter, Fiona, to Canada. He believed they would be safer there. But Gunda and Garth's marriage did not last. They divorced, and Williams decided to make a fresh start in America.

A British Red Cross ambulance crew helps people during World War II. This is the kind of work Williams did during the war.

Try Garth Williams

Williams arrived in New York City in 1941. The Japanese Air Force attacked Pearl Harbor, Hawaii, just ten days later. The attack drew the United States into **World War II**. To earn money, Williams advised companies about **camouflage**. He also worked in a lens-making factory for a while.

Williams returned to the art world in 1943. He sold drawings to the famous *New Yorker* magazine. The magazine sometimes rejected his cartoons, however. The editors said his style was too wild.

Williams decided to try a different market for his artwork. He showed his **portfolio** to Ursula Nordstrom. She was an editor of children's books at the publisher Harper & Row. Nordstrom was just starting work on a new book from author E.B. White. Many artists wanted to illustrate this book.

The author was already familiar with Williams's work, however. White sent his **manuscript** for *Stuart Little* to

Nordstrom with a handwritten note. It read, "Try Garth Williams."

Suddenly, there was no competition to illustrate the book. The job belonged to Williams. With White's charming story and the playful lines of Williams's illustrations, *Stuart Little* was a big success.

Jonathan Lipnicki, star of the movie **Stuart Little,** *holds White's book.*

Elements of Art

Line

Line is one of the most basic parts of art. Lines are used to define a particular form. Williams's illustrations primarily used lines. He created them with a simple pencil.

Pencils are usually made of graphite or charcoal. The marks of charcoal pencils can be smudged for shading. Artists can erase or smudge the markings of graphite pencils, too. But, graphite is not as dusty. The graphite in drawing pencils comes in a range of hardness levels for different effects.

Full-Time Artist

Stuart Little was the first of many successful projects for Williams. In 1945, he met author Margaret Wise Brown. Brown is best known for writing *Goodnight Moon*. Williams and Brown worked well together. Their partnership resulted in 11 books, including *The Sailor Dog*, *Mister Dog*, and *Home for a Bunny.*

Williams remarried in 1947. His new wife's name was Dorothea. The two lived on a farm in New York. The farm inspired many drawings for Williams's 1952 project with E.B. White, *Charlotte's Web*. The farm would also serve as inspiration for Williams's next big project.

Ursula Nordstrom wanted Williams to illustrate a series of books by Laura Ingalls Wilder. The books were about a young girl's experience as an American pioneer in the 1870s and 1880s. Williams was not used to drawing people, but Nordstrom urged him to try it. He eventually agreed and got to work.

Later in life, Williams visited the home of Laura Ingalls Wilder many times. He said he admired that she knew the meaning of hardship.

The Little House Books

Williams knew little about pioneer life. So, he began a six-month journey. He drove west to Mansfield, Missouri, and met Laura Ingalls Wilder and her husband, Almanzo.

Williams often visited libraries to talk with children about Wilder's books.

Williams also visited the places mentioned in Wilder's books. He went to Minnesota and South Dakota. He tried to see the land through Wilder's eyes. He knew she had lived in a **sod** house as a child. An adult might see a sod house as dirty and ugly. But, Williams knew that a child might like it.

The Little House books would be an eight-volume series. Originally, Williams was asked to do color paintings for the books. The publishers soon decided that was too expensive. They settled on pencil sketches for the books instead.

The Little House drawings were done on tracing paper. They all had to be the same small size as they would be when printed. This led to Williams getting his first pair of eyeglasses.

Some authors had a lot to say about what they wanted for illustrations. Wilder did not. She was helpful whenever Williams needed information. But, she trusted him. She never asked him to change anything. The Little House books were published in 1953.

Williams visits the childhood home of Laura Ingalls Wilder in South Dakota while researching the Little House series.

The Rabbits' Wedding

Williams took on many more projects in the 1950s. He worked with Simon & Schuster to illustrate titles for their Golden Books series. He created the art for more than 20 other children's books. He also illustrated six books he wrote himself.

Williams looks at the awards he has won for his many projects.

One of these was called *The Rabbits' Wedding*. Williams wrote the book in 1958. It is the story of two rabbits who marry and live in the forest. One of the rabbits is black. The other rabbit is white.

Some people were upset with *The Rabbits' Wedding*. They believed in **segregation**. These people thought Williams was saying white and black people should get married. They disagreed so much that they banned his book from many libraries.

Williams explained why he had drawn one rabbit white and the other black. He said publishers at that time found color printing very expensive. That meant he could use only black and white drawings. Still, the conflict over *The Rabbits' Wedding* made headlines in newspapers around the world.

Though Williams gave a simple reason for the colors in **The Rabbits' Wedding,** *the book was removed from library shelves in the state of Alabama.*

Settling in Mexico

In the late 1950s, Williams bought land in Mexico. The land included the ruins of a Spanish castle and a silver mine. Williams fixed up the 400-year-old castle and turned it into his new home.

The house included a large studio where he could draw and paint. In 1960, Williams illustrated Russell Hoban's *Bedtime for Frances*. He also drew the pictures for George Selden's *The Cricket in Times Square*.

Williams's wife Dorothea died in 1965. He soon married for a third time. However, that marriage ended in divorce. Williams then met a Mexican woman named Leticia. The two married in 1974. Leticia helped organize the thousands of pieces of artwork Williams had created.

Williams was still illustrating books in his seventies and eighties. He used new art styles and techniques whenever he could. He experimented with color and texture.

For example, he used many brilliant colors when illustrating *Beneath a Blue Umbrella* by Jack Prelutsky. *The New York*

Times chose it as one of the ten best illustrated books of 1990. This was one of Williams's last projects.

Garth Williams died at his home in Mexico on May 8, 1996. He was 84 years old. Children all over the world still enjoy his illustrations. He remains one of the most well respected illustrators of children's books.

Garth Williams's home in Mexico

Glossary

architecture - the art of planning and designing buildings. A person who designs architecture is called an architect.

camouflage - a pattern designed to blend into the surroundings for disguise.

dictator - a ruler with complete control who usually governs in a cruel or unfair way.

Great Depression - a period (from 1929 to 1942) of worldwide economic trouble when there was little buying or selling, and many people could not find work.

headmaster - the principal of a private school.

landscape - a painting that shows a stretch of scenery.

manuscript - a book or article written by hand or typed before being published.

portfolio - a portable case holding a collection of an artist's work for display.

segregation - the separation of an individual or a group from a larger group.

sod - a rectangular section of grass held together by roots.

World War II - from 1939 to 1945, fought in Europe, Asia, and Africa. Great Britain, France, the United States, the Soviet Union, and their allies were on one side. Germany, Italy, Japan, and their allies were on the other side.

Web Sites

To learn more about Garth Williams, visit ABDO Publishing Company on the World Wide Web at **www.abdopub.com**. Web sites about Garth Williams are featured on our Book Links page. These links are roulinely monitored and updated to provide the most current information available.

Index